Khala's Little Din

Written by Hanaa Unus
Illustrated by Hazel Quintanilla

Khala's Little Dinosaur/ by Hanaa Unus
ISBN-13: 978-1500318819
ISBN-10: 1500318817

Printed in the U.S.A

For
the newest of the bunch Rabia, Aaira, and
Maryam. And for Ibrahim, Ayyoob, Rumaysa,
Zahra, and Bayan.

Dear Little
Dinosaur,
I love you so!

Dear Little Dinosaur,
I pray for you each
day,

that Allah keeps you safe,

that He gives you good health,

and sends happiness your way.

Dear Little Dinosaur,
if only you knew,

just how much pride I have in you.

Dear Little Dinosaur, with the simplest of play,

somehow you whisk
all my worries away.

Dear Little Dinosaur, though at times you fuss and fight,

for you I am truly grateful
each night.

Dear Little Dinosaur,
you've grown so tall,

just as my love has
since those first days
when you were so small.

Dear Little Dinosaur, I love our little talks,

but most of all I love when you hold my hand on our walks.

Dear Little
Dinosaur,
know that
whatever
life sends,

a Khala's love never ends.

More children's reading by this author

'Oh, the Things an Aunt Will Do'   'Oh, the Things a Khala Will Do'

Made in the USA
Charleston, SC
25 July 2014